VICKI COBB
SCIENCE PLAY

I Face
the
Wind

by Vicki Cobb
illustrated by Julia Gorton

HarperCollins Publishers

For Jillian Davis Cobb
—V.C.

To the teachers at Forest Avenue
School in Glen Ridge, New Jersey
—J.G.

The author gratefully acknowledges
Dr. Myra Zarnowsky of Queens College for her help
in making this series developmentally appropriate.

I Face the Wind
Text copyright © 2003 by Vicki Cobb
Illustrations copyright © 2003 by Julia Gorton
Manufactured in China. All rights reserved.
For information address HarperCollins Children's
Books, a division of HarperCollins Publishers,
195 Broadway, New York, NY 10007.
www.harperchildrens.com

Library of Congress Cataloging-in-Publication Data
Cobb, Vicki.
  I face the wind / by Vicki Cobb ; illustrated by Julia Gorton.
    p.   cm.
  Summary: Introduces the characteristics and actions of the wind through
simple hands-on activities.
  ISBN 0-688-17840-5 — ISBN 0-688-17841-3 (lib. bdg.)
  1. Wind—Juvenile literature. 2. Wind—Experiments—Juvenile literature. [1.
Wind. 2. Wind—Experiments. 3. Experiments.] I. Gorton, Julia, ill. II. Title.
QC931.4 .C63 2003   2001026480
551.51'8'078—dc21   CIP
                                                                                AC

Typography by Julia Gorton
15 16 17 18 SCP 20 19 18 17 16
First Edition

Note to the Reader

This book is designed so that your child can make discoveries. It poses a series of questions that can be answered by doing activities that temporarily take the child away from the book. The best way to use this book is to do the activities, without rushing, as they come up during your reading. You will have to help with some of the activities, such as blowing up balloons and tying them. Turn the page to the next part of the text only after the child has made the discovery. That way, the book will reinforce what the child has found out through experience. Before you begin reading this book to your child, have on hand a wire coat hanger, a pencil, a large (grocery) plastic bag, two identical balloons or two gallon-size zip-close plastic bags, tape, and a ball.

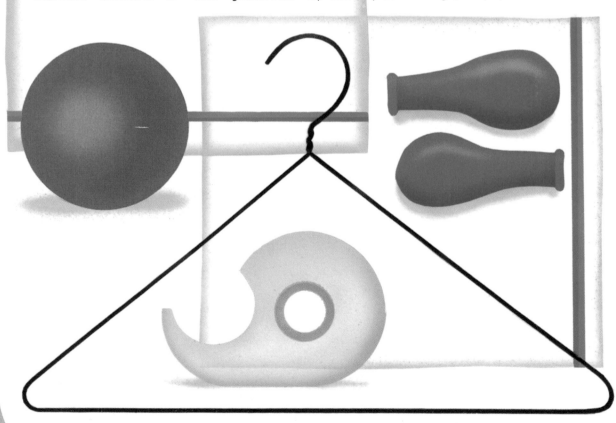

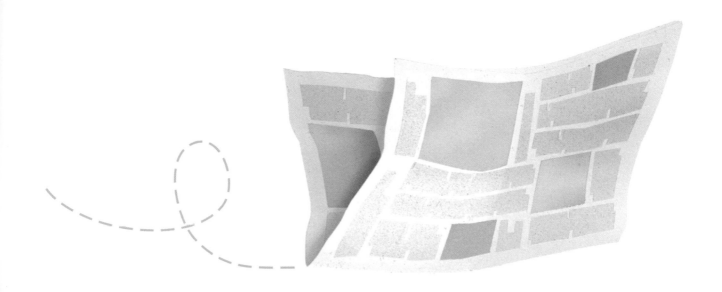

Ever face a strong wind?

Your hair blows away
from your face.
You could lose your hat.
And if the wind is
blowing hard enough,
you may even have
to walk at a slant.

You can't see this force that's pushing you. But you can feel it. And you can see what wind does to other things.

It makes dust swirl in a circle.

It makes flags stick out straight and flutter.

Can you name some things you see wind do?

Go outside and watch.

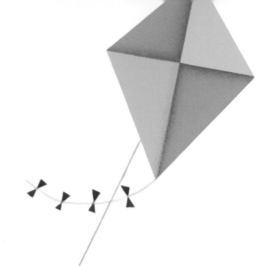

A kite stays in the sky.

AN UMBRELLA TURNS INSIDE OUT.

Add your own ideas to the list.

Why does the wind push you?

You can discover why by asking questions and doing things to get answers. Here's the first question. What is wind made of?

Wind is made of air. You can't see air.
But you can catch it. Here's how.
Open a large plastic bag.
Make sure there are no holes in it.
Pull it through the air so it puffs up.

Twist it closed to trap the air you caught. If it is closed so that it is airtight, you can squeeze the bag with the air in it and feel the air push back at you as you squeeze.

Air is real stuff.
It is just as real as this book or

A BOWL OF SOUP.

Like all real stuff,

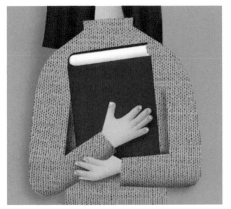  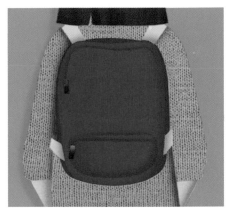

AIR is heavier than nothing.

How can you weigh air? You can't weigh air like you weigh yourself. It's so very light. You can weigh air by doing an experiment.

You will need

a coat hanger,
a pencil,
two identical balloons
or large
zip-close plastic bags,
and tape.

1 Hang the coat hanger on the pencil.

2 Pull one side down and let go.

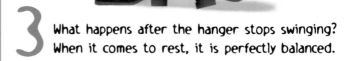

3 What happens after the hanger stops swinging?
When it comes to rest, it is perfectly balanced.

You can weigh things on a balanced hanger.

Tape an empty balloon or zip-close plastic bag
to each side of the hanger.

The hanger is balanced because
both balloons or bags weigh the same.

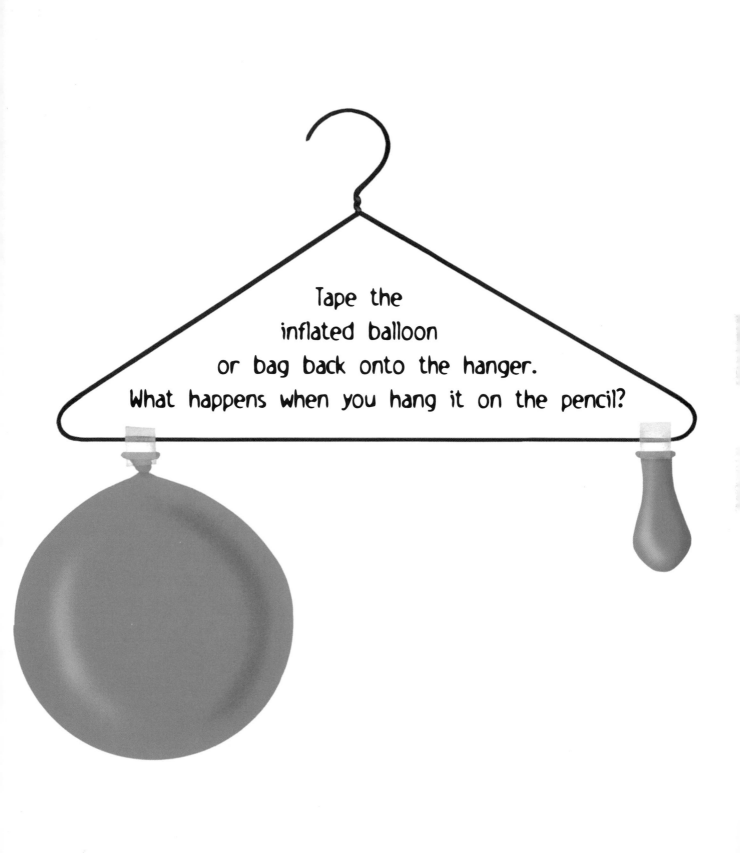

Tape the
inflated balloon
or bag back onto the hanger.
What happens when you hang it on the pencil?

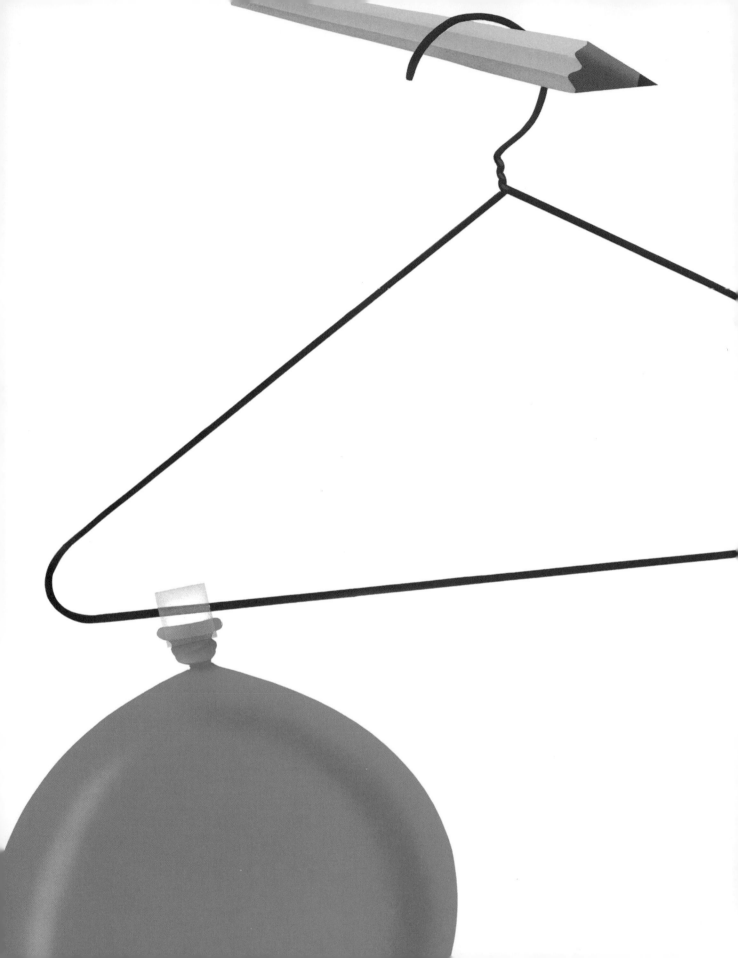

The hanger is slightly tilted again!
It is tilted only a little bit because
air doesn't weigh very much. Even so,
the side containing air is heavier than
the side that has the empty balloon or bag.
This proves that air has weight.

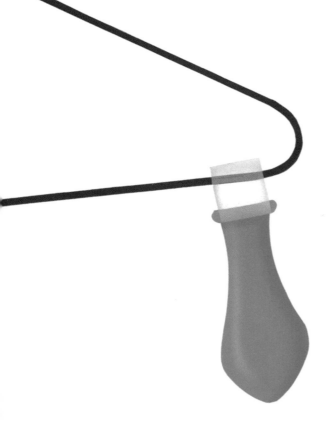

But the weight of air is only part of the reason that you feel wind.
Air is made of a gazillion tiny balls floating in space.

These balls are so small that they can't be seen. They have to be imagined. They are called molecules. Wind is made of moving air molecules.

Imagine that a ball is like a single moving air molecule. Sit on the floor and roll a ball so that it bumps into your leg.

Can you feel it push against you?

Roll it quickly into your leg.

Roll it slowly into your leg.

Which makes a stronger bump?

How can you make
air molecules move?

Wave this book.

The book pushes against
the air molecules and
starts them moving.
Then they push on you
and you feel it.

Wave it slowly.

Wave the book quickly.

Which wind is stronger?

Are there other ways you can make wind?

Blow air out of your mouth.
Wave your hand in front of your face.
Be an inventor and make your
own kind of air movers.

The faster the air moves, the stronger the wind. The fastest winds of all are in a tornado. These winds are so strong they can lift a roof right off a house or make a truck fly through the air.

One of the
softest winds
is your breath.
Put your fingertips
near your nose
and feel your
soft breath.

When you face
the wind,
gazillions of
moving air molecules
collide with you.
That's why you
feel the push
of the wind.

Yay!